Would you like help on an "impossible" project? Send an email briefly describing your project to **kimberly@SiliconValleyAlliances.com**, and we can set up a time for a FREE fifteen-minute "conversation for possibilities." Woohoo! EXCITING! – Kimberly

Inspired Organizational Cultures

エンゲージメントを高める組織文化

Discover Your DNA, Engage Your People,
and Design Your Future

by Kimberly Wiefling

Foreword by Dr. Edgar Schein

An Actionable Business Journal

E-mail: info@thinkaha.com
20660 Stevens Creek Blvd., Suite 210
Cupertino, CA 95014

Published by THiNKaha®
20660 Stevens Creek Blvd., Suite 210, Cupertino, CA 95014
http://thinkaha.com
E-mail: info@thinkaha.com

First Printing: March 2018
Hardcover ISBN: 978-1-61699-225-5 (1-61699-225-5)
Paperback ISBN: 978-1-61699-134-0 (1-61699-134-8)
eBook ISBN: 978-1-61699-135-7 (1-61699-135-6)
Place of Publication: Silicon Valley, California, USA
Paperback Library of Congress Number: 2014945330

Trademarks

Warning and Disclaimer

Advance Praise

"Kimberly has helped our company shape its global culture for the past decade. To date, over 350 colleagues from around the world [have] met together for six-month customized programs consisting of three one-week interactive sessions in our Global Team Leadership Development program. Our culture is rooted in a long history of innovative change to survive in the face of global business headwinds. We have successfully transformed our company many times in the past 90 years, but mainly as a Japanese company. As we invest more around the world, these transformations become more difficult. It may not be 'cause and effect,' but our company has significantly increased its global businesses outside of Japan and is performing at record levels, concurrent with our collaboration with Kimberly."

George Avdey
President & CEO, Kuraray America, Inc.

"You can leave it up to Kimberly Wiefling to, in 140-bite-sized quotes, show you how to stay true to your core values while leaping forward to an engaged and purposeful future. In her trademark entertaining way, Kimberly has taken her over 25 years of experience with companies worldwide and provided you with a step-by-step guide to design your organization's culture in a way that creates real and lasting impact for your teams and your organization."

Nathalie Udo
InDepth Strategies, CEO, and author of *Organizational Survival: Profitable Strategies for a Sustainable Future*

"We learned from Kimberly's sessions how important it is for each employee to understand our company's organizational DNA. I believe that the bond developed between overseas employees through understanding our shared DNA will result in leading our global business into the future in spite of their different backgrounds, cultures, and nationalities."

Chihiro Sato
Pigeon Group

"Kimberly's organizational culture work with us was like a journey to discover the hidden common sense shared in our organization and people across the world. Our company's leaders successfully discovered their instinct and got much more unified as One Global Family after the journey. You can see some images of the journey from this book, just like reading a travel guidebook before taking off."

Shinya Kimura
Yamaha Motor Co., Ltd

"Keep Kimberly's *Inspired Organizational Cultures* within arm's reach. It is filled with many thought-provoking tips and sage advice intended to make us think about what was, is, and could be in our organizations. This book explores organizational culture from a variety of perspectives, but always with the intention of inspiring positive opportunities for meaningful growth. Focus on any of the 140 nuggets and allow your mind to wander and explore within the context of your personal experience."

Kerstin Lynam
Chief People Officer, Velo3D

Dedication

This book is dedicated to my mentor, Dr. Edgar Schein, who has awoken in me the realization that the work I've been doing all of my life has been subject to the inescapable, but not unalterable, tractor beam of organizational culture.

Acknowledgement

How on Earth did this book finally get written and published? It lay 90 percent finished and dormant for years!

It was inspired by dozens of talented colleagues and hundreds of fascinating encounters with valued clients.

It was translated by Naomi Kazusa, a wonderful friend with a talent for "interpretation beyond words."

It was guided by the most amazing mentor I have ever had the privilege to know, Dr. Edgar Schein. Very much alive at the age of ninety-ish, he has deepened my understanding of what it means to transform individuals, teams, and organizations.

And it was finally birthed into being by the patient encouragement of my publisher, Mitchell Levy, and the tireless persistence of the incredible Jenilee Maniti.

I am also deeply appreciative of my wonderful friend Kimiko Arimoto who contributed advice crucial to the formatting of the Japanese portions of this book.

The seeds of this book were planted when my Japanese sister, Yuko Shibata, boldly declared that I could facilitate workshops on corporate culture and organizational DNA for our globalizing Japanese clients. As always, she believed in me more than I believed in myself. Well, what do you know? We were wildly successful in helping our clients transform their cultures from invisible to visible, tangible, and actionable.

Thank you to all my co-conspirators in our Consulting Collaboratory, my partners in Japan—now spread to the four winds—and especially my tribe at Silicon Valley Alliances (http://www.siliconvalleyalliances.com/)!

Why I Wrote This Book

I wrote *Inspired Organizational Cultures* to demystify the elusive concept of organizational culture and to continue to support the work that I do best—enabling organizations to achieve what SEEMS impossible, but is merely difficult. My deep experience working with globalizing Japanese companies worldwide makes this book highly relevant to anyone who is determined to build effective teams across borders and boundaries of every kind in pursuit of business success. A physicist by education, I realized long ago the limits of technology devoid of human skills—the so-called "touchy feely" aspects of working in teams so vital to success, and so frequently overlooked.

Don't just make a living, make a difference!

Kimberly Wiefling

http://www.SiliconValleyAlliances.com

http://www.wiefling.com

http://www.KimberlyWiefling.com

http://inspiredcompanyculture.com/

http://scrappyprojectmanagement.com/

http://possibilitiestoolbox.com/

http://scrappydesignthinking.com/

https://www.facebook.com/WieflingConsulting

kimberly@wiefling.com

#kwiefling

How to Read a THiNKaha® Book
A Note from the Publisher

The THiNKaha series is the CliffsNotes of the 21st century. The value of these books is that they are contextual in nature. Although the actual words won't change, their meaning will change every time you read one as your context will change. Experience your own "AHA!" moments ("AHAmessages™") with a THiNKaha book; AHAmessages are looked at as "actionable" moments—think of a specific project you're working on, an event, a sales deal, a personal issue, etc. and see how the AHAmessages in this book can inspire your own AHAmessages, something that you can specifically act on. Here's how to read one of these books and have it work for you:

1. Read a THiNKaha book (these slim and handy books should only take about 15–20 minutes of your time!) and write down one to three actionable items you thought of while reading it. Each journal-style THiNKaha book is equipped with space for you to write down your notes and thoughts underneath each AHAmessage.

2. Mark your calendar to re-read this book again in 30 days.

3. Repeat step #1 and write down one to three more AHAmessages that grab you this time. I guarantee that they will be different than the first time. BTW: this is also a great time to reflect on the actions taken from the last set of AHAmessages you wrote down.

After reading a THiNKaha book, writing down your AHAmessages, re-reading it, and writing down more AHAmessages, you'll begin to see how these books contextually apply to you. THiNKaha books advocate for continuous, lifelong learning. They will help you transform your AHAs into actionable items with tangible results until you no longer have to say "AHA!" to these moments—they'll become part of your daily practice as you continue to grow and learn.

As The AHA Guy at THiNKaha, I definitely practice what I preach. I read 2-3 AHAbooks a month in addition to those that we publish and take away two to three different action items from each of them every time. Please e-mail me your AHAs today!

Mitchell Levy
publisher@thinkaha.com

Contents

Foreword

Organizational culture is very much "in" but not well understood, often trivialized, and rarely analyzed in a systematic way. This "workbook" is a wonderful vehicle for overcoming all of these flaws. This book leads you into the topic of culture step by step, educating you as you go along so that you not only understand the depth of culture but have begun a valid analysis of the culture you are living in and co-creating.

What makes this book especially relevant is that it has been produced by a consultant who has had a wealth of experience in different organizations and, more importantly, in different national cultures, especially in Japan. The process which this book invites can be used on one's work group, one's employing organization, or one's nation with equal profit. Kimberly should be congratulated for providing us a culture-deciphering process that will be widely used and with great profit.

Edgar H. Schein
Professor Emeritus, MIT Sloan School of Management
Author of *Organizational Culture and Leadership, 5th ed. (2017)* and *Humble Consulting (2017)*.

Introduction
Design Your Organization's Culture

There's a global epidemic of organizational dysfunctionality. Employee engagement scores in the US are around 33% on average, and worldwide they are 15%! Japan has one of the lowest employee engagement scores of the ~140 countries that Gallup surveys, with a mere 6%. Regrettably, most organizations are failing for entirely predictable and avoidable reasons.

Behaviors that contribute to this sorry state of affairs include:
- employees' over-reliance on email
- managers distracting themselves with busywork instead of focusing on the organization's most important priorities
- failure to build trusting relationships as the foundation of working together effectively.
- teams with unclear goals, unclear communication, and unclear priorities
- organizations where the org chart has become irrelevant, but people haven't mastered the concepts of influencing stakeholders across borders and boundaries of every kind.

Research on global teams by an MIT professor showed that 82% of global teams studied considered their teams to have failed, and the top reasons were:
- failure to build trust
- failure to overcome communication barriers
- goals of team members and the team were not aligned
- goals and vision of the team were unclear.

While many business leaders focus on strategy, structure and culture are even more powerful influencers of business outcomes. I strongly believe that the types of failures listed above are designed into the structures and cultures of many organizations. This may be one reason why companies like Morningstar, W.L. Gore, Valve, and Semco have rejected traditional ways of organizing their companies and managing their businesses.

Strategy simply isn't enough to overcome an organization that is designed to fail. Peter Drucker famously said, "Culture eats strategy for breakfast."

But what is this fluffy concept called "culture"? An organization's culture consists of the patterns of assumptions, beliefs, expectations, and taboos that define "reality" and shape the collective behavior of people operating in that organization. It's "the way we do things around here" even if we've forgotten why we're doing it. Like the air we breathe, it's largely unnoticed but ever-present, and it strongly influences the way that people interact with each other and the external world. Flout those norms, and you'll find that culture can be as strong as cement and tougher to alter than your spouse's irritating lifelong habits.

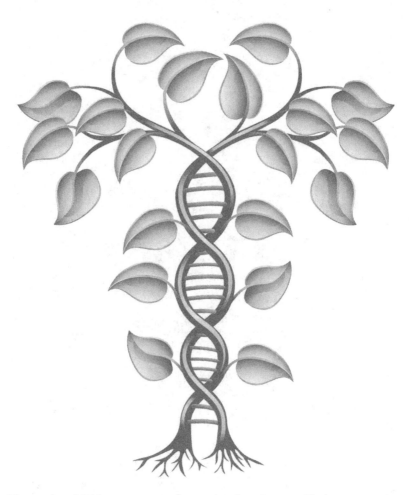

Share the AHA messages from this book socially by going to
http://aha.pub/InspiredOrgCultures

Section I
Discover Your Organization's Cultural DNA

An organization's "cultural DNA" is a property of its culture and the historical basis of these norms—the "genetic code" at the root of an organization's culture. Most every kid who has the luxury of getting an education learns the basics of biological DNA. It's what causes a giraffe to have a long neck, kangaroos to have pouches, and porcupines to have quills instead of fur. Tadpoles turn into frogs, not butterflies, because of their DNA. Even behavior has its roots in an organism's genetic code. Birds have wings, but dogs don't, therefore dogs don't fly. Snakes, lacking both legs and wings, resort to crawling. But what is the meaning of the DNA of an *organization*?

Like the DNA of plants and animals, our organization's cultural DNA influences who we are and how we behave. Although we can change our individual and group behaviors, our DNA defines the core of our identity, and sets boundaries on who we can become. A dog that's been abused might bark aggressively and bite humans, but it won't start eating worms, tweeting, or building a nest out of twigs!

Discover the unique identity of your organization by exploring your organization's culture and its cultural DNA. Exploring your past together will provide a solid foundation for creating a shared future.

1

DNA isn't just for humans. Organizations share a cultural genetic code that makes them unique and binds their people together.

DNAは人間だけにあるものではない。
組織もそれぞれ独自の文化を持ち、
その遺伝子はそこで働く人々を結びつける。

_____

_____

_____

2

An organization's culture and DNA define its identity. They're the roots of who you are, what you stand for, and how you behave.

あなたが属する組織のDNAと文化が、組織の
アイデンティティの決め手となり、あなたが何者か、
何を支持するか、どうふるまうかの基礎となる。

_____

_____

_____

3

An organization's DNA is inherited, but it isn't static.
Just as in nature, beneficial mutations help
you change and evolve.

組織のDNAは受け継がれていくが、
常に同じ状態ではない。自然と同様、
有用な突然変異が組織の変化と進化を促す。

_____

_____

_____

4

Your history doesn't limit what you can become.
DNA and organizations inevitably change over time.
Change for the better!

組織の歴史は変化を制限するものではない。
DNAも組織も、時が経つにつれて必然的に変わって
いく。よりよい方向に変わろう！

_____

_____

_____

5

An organization's DNA is the common thread that ties your people together, connecting your history to your future possibilities.

組織のDNAは内部の人々をつなぐ糸であり、組織の歴史と将来の可能性をつなぐ共通基盤である。

_____

_____

_____

6

Your organization's DNA planted the seeds of your brand. It's what makes you unique. It's the difference you make.

組織のDNAがブランドの種を蒔く。DNAは組織の独自性を示し、社会変革を起こす力を持つ。

_____

_____

_____

7

People love an organization with purpose, strong core
values, and guiding principles. Discover these
in your cultural DNA.

人を惹きつけてやまない組織には明確な目的があり、
しっかりとした中核的価値観や指針がある。自分が
属する組織の文化のDNAからそれらを探し出そう。

_____

_____

_____

8

An organization's DNA doesn't dictate what the future holds. You have the power to reshape your culture and alter your destiny.

DNAは組織の未来を決定づけるものではない。
あなたには組織の文化を再構築する力がある。
それで組織の運命を変えるのだ。

9

The beauty of organizational DNA is that it provides support while being flexible. Preserve the best and change the rest!

組織のDNAの素晴らしさは、人々を支える枠組みでありながら、柔軟性に富んでいることだ。
最も良いものだけを残し、他は変えていこう!

10

An organization's DNA is a metaphor for your unique identity, and the internal foundation of an authentic external brand.

組織のDNAとは、その組織独自のアイデンテイテイの比喩表現であり、本物のブランドを対外的に発信するための組織内部の基礎である。

_____

_____

_____

11

Exploring your organization's DNA reminds people that you share an identity that will persist despite fleeting controversy.

組織のDNA探求を通じて人々は、
葛藤を経て生き残ったアイデンテイテイを
他者と共有していることを思い出す。

_____

_____

_____

12

Your organization's DNA can be the source
of your strength or the seeds of your demise.
If you want more roses, plant more roses!

DNAは組織の強みの源となる場合もあれば、
組織の消滅をもたらす種となる場合もある。
バラの花をたくさん咲かせたければ、
バラの種をもっと植えよう!

_____

_____

_____

13

Exploring your cultural DNA opens the door to
endless possibilities to fully leverage the past
and imagine a brighter future.

組織の文化のDNAを探ることで無限の可能性への
ドアが開かれ、過去の遺産を活かして明るい未来を
描けるようになる。

_____

_____

_____

14

Achieving temporary success is great,
but having cultural DNA that continuously inspires
your people is a lasting treasure.

成功をおさめることは（たとえ一時的であっても）
すばらしい。だが継続的に人々を鼓舞する文化の
DNAを確立すれば、それは永遠の宝となる。

_____

_____

_____

15

Becoming deeply familiar with your organization's
DNA increases the potential for breakthroughs
and sustainable success.

自分が属する組織のDNAに精通することで突破口が
開かれ、持続可能な成功につながる可能性が高まる。

_____

_____

_____

16

An organization's DNA is the common history that unifies your people. It's the "roots of the fruits" that you produce together.

組織のDNAはそこで働く人々の共通の歴史であり、彼らを一つにまとめる役割を果たす。皆で作り上げる「果実の根」である。

_____

_____

_____

17

Each organization manifests a unique culture with its own style. Enhance yours through exploring your cultural DNA.

どの組織も独自のスタイルを有する文化を打ち出している。自分が属する組織の文化のDNAを探り、独自の文化を強化しよう。

_____

_____

_____

18

Deeply understanding your cultural DNA leads to knowing your organization's purpose, why it exists, and why it matters.

自分が属する組織の文化のDNAを深く理解することは組織の目的と存在意義を知ることにつながる。

_____

_____

_____

19

How can you understand others if you don't understand
yourself? Raise your self-awareness to better understand
your organization.

自らを理解せずして他者を理解することはできない。
自己認識を高めて自分の属する組織への理解を深め
よう。

_____

_____

_____

Share the AHA messages from this book socially by going to
http://aha.pub/InspiredOrgCultures

Section II
Journey Through Your History Together

An organization's founders' stories often inspire admiration. Tales of courageous risk-taking, determination in the face of overwhelming odds, or staunch commitment to a purpose beyond profit can unite people around this heritage. Here are a few of my favorites from my clients in the corporate world:

- Yamaha - In 1887, Torakusu Yamaha built his first reed organ and carried it on his back over the mountains of Japan to the music university in Tokyo. Unfortunately, it was flatly rejected due to its poor tuning! Undaunted, Torakusu created an improved version and carried it back to Tokyo once again on this torturous journey. This organ became the foundation of the Yamaha music business.
- Kuraray - Magosaburo Ohara founded Kuraray in 1926, and his son Soichiro Ohara continued their legacy of "contributing to the world and individual well-being through actions that others are unable to produce."[1] I find myself quoting Mr. Ohara's sage advice to teams stuck in "death by consensus": "To initiate a project one has to begin when only one or two of ten people are in favor of it."[2]
- Suntory - In 1899, Shinjiro Torii opened a wine shop in Osaka, and—despite the warnings of naysayers—proceeded to produce a popular port wine domestically. Later, Suntory was the first company to distill whiskey in Japan. Of course, many people declared that it was impossible to make a great whiskey there, but his "Yatte Minahare!" spirit (roughly translated as "Go for it!") prevailed.

What treasures are hidden in your organization's history? Stories of enormous success are valuable, but so are those of how people responded when faced with overwhelming challenges or setbacks.

What epic moments from your organization's past are worthy of being preserved and transmitted to future generations? Journey together to the roots of your organization's cultural DNA through the power of historical storytelling.

---

1. Fumio Ito, "Message from the President," *kuraray*, http://www.kuraray.co.jp/en/company/president/.
2. George Avdey, "Building a Global Business: November 2014 Update for Customer Service" (PowerPoint presentation, Kuraray America, Inc., 2014).

20

A powerful way to understand what's happening today is to look back and reflect on the truth of what happened yesterday.

今何が起きているかを理解するには、
過去を振り返って現実に何が起きたかを考えるのが
効果的である。

_____

_____

_____

21

Each organization has historical DNA that contributed to its present culture and influences its future possibilities.

それぞれの組織における過去のDNAは、現在の文化に
貢献し、将来の可能性に影響を与える。

_____

_____

_____

22

Moving forward is challenging when you don't know where you're headed, but your organization's past can guide you to your future.

自分がどの方向に進んでいるかわからずに前進する
ことは難しい。しかし自分が属する組織の過去が
将来へと導いてくれる。

23

Understanding your past clarifies your present and your purpose. That's what exploring your cultural DNA is all about.

自らの過去を理解することで現在の自分とその目的が明らかになる。組織の文化のDNAを探るというのはつまりそういうことだ。

_____
_____
_____

24

Get to know the history of each of your team members. You are on a journey together. Dare to wander, explore, and discover.

自分が属するチームのメンバーの過去を知ろう。ともに旅路を歩む仲間だ。勇気を出してさまよい歩き、探検し、発見しよう。

_____
_____
_____

25

Encourage your team to explore the history of your organization to discover and interpret the roots of your shared identity.

チームメンバーに組織の歴史を探るよう促そう。
皆が共有するアイデンテイテイのルーツを見つけ、
考察させよう。

26

Having a shared sense of history and shared values enables your organization to stick together when addressing serious problems.

共通の歴史認識と価値観を持つことで組織が深刻な
問題に対処する時の結束力が高まる。

27

If you don't know your organization's past,
and you don't understand your present,
you'll struggle to create your future.

自分が属する組織の過去を知らず、現在を理解して
いなければ、未来を創り出すことは難しい。

_____

_____

_____

28

Every organization has a purpose. Go on a
journey to discover the reason you exist.
Take the time to redefine what matters most.

組織にはそれぞれ目的がある。自分が属する組織の
存在理由を見つける旅に出よう。時間をとって、
一番重要なことは何かをあらためて明確にしよう。

29

Exploring your cultural DNA requires that you look at not
only the positive things about it, but the dark side as well.

自分が属する組織の文化のDNA探求にあたっては、
明るい面ばかりでなく暗い面も見る必要がある。

30

Exploring the history of your organization casts a
light in the direction of future possibilities.
Start to light the way today.

自分が属する組織の歴史を調べることは、将来の
可能性への道筋に光を当てることになる。
その道を今日から照らそう。

_____

_____

_____

31

Bring people together to explore your organization's
history. A common understanding of your past
inspires a shared future.

皆で力を合わせて組織の歴史を探ろう。
過去について共通理解を得ることが、
ともに未来を描くためのいい刺激になる。

_____

_____

_____

32

To live and breathe your organization's culture,
understand the roots of its existence, its core purpose,
its reason for being.

組織の文化を自分のものにして実践するには、
組織のルーツ、主な目的、存在理由を
理解しなくてはならない。

_____

_____

_____

33

Your past is the foundation of your future, not a prison.
In organizations, as in life, it's never too late to change.

過去は人が永遠に囚われる場所ではなく、
未来を切り開く基盤である。人の人生と同じように、
組織も変わるのに遅すぎるということはない。

_____

_____

_____

34

Don't underestimate the power of discovering your organization's history. It can powerfully shape your people's sense of purpose.

組織の歴史をひもとくことの意義を過小評価してはならない。それによって人々の目的意識を形成することができるからである。

_____

_____

_____

Share the AHA messages from this book socially by going to
http://aha.pub/InspiredOrgCultures

Section III
Learn from Your Past, the Greats, and Each Other

DNA isn't destiny. Mutations occur naturally, scientists intentionally create genetic modifications, and reproduction combines genes in ways that create new and sometimes surprising results. Environmental factors can impact gene expression. Genetically identical caterpillars exposed to different colors of light developed dramatic differences in wing color as they grew into butterflies. The old paradigm of "genetic determinism" is being replaced with the idea that genes respond to information—from both external environments and cognitive (internal) environments. Likewise, organizations are subject to external influences, and some do find ways to break free of their historical roots rather than become extinct. Organizations, like organisms, can learn and evolve.

Learn from the founders and historical roots of your organization. But, for cryin' out loud, don't rush over to your PR department to pick up a stack of those glossy brochures containing the company history and poignant stories of the founders. Passing them out will only cause people to roll their eyes, and they're pretty much guaranteed to go straight into the recycling bin. And don't be trapped by the past! You might have been born with straight black hair, but you can dye it platinum blond and get a perm if you like.

Learn from great examples, but don't simply transplant best practices from other organizations to yours. Grafting a unicorn's head onto a scorpion is unlikely to produce a unicorn. That's essentially what some companies do when they try to copy best practices from other companies. Installing a cappuccino machine and foosball table in the cafeteria of a stodgy old firm won't make people more innovative, and instituting "The Toyota Way" in a political shark tank won't empower individuals to "kaizen" their jobs away.

Learn from each other. An organization's culture is propagated through stories. Collect and preserve the best of them like treasures. Create forums where people are invited to share stories that contribute to the evolution of your organization's culture.

Building and sustaining a healthy organizational culture isn't a temporary project. Like maintaining good hygiene, it's a job that's never truly finished and must be repeated daily.

35

Not all lessons are found in books. The most inspiring ones are found in your own people's history, experiences, and stories.

教訓が見つかるのは本の中だけではない。
最も感動を与える教訓は組織で働く人々の歴史、
経験、物語の中にある。

_____

_____

_____

36

Stories of people who persevered against enormous
odds to achieve great success are inspiring.
Listen to them. Learn from them.

逆境の中で苦労のすえに大成功をおさめた人々の
物語には胸打たれるものがある。
耳を傾け、学びを得よう。

_____

_____

_____

37

You don't need to look far to find inspiring people.
Everyday heroes walk among us. We find what we look for -
so start LOOKING!

感動を与えてくれる人々を遠くまで探しに行く
必要はない。
毎日、私たちが歩いている雑踏の中に英雄がいる。
意識して探せばきっと見つかる。

_____

_____

_____

38

When charting your direction, use your organization's guiding principles as your compass. Navigate by your values, not just value.

今後の方向性を見定める時、組織の指針を
磁石代わりに使おう。単なる金銭的価値でなく、
価値基準に従って行動しよう。

_____

_____

_____

39

Live up to the legacy of your organization's founders. Their history planted the seeds of today's success and tomorrow's promise.

組織の創設者たちが残した遺産に恥じない行動を
しよう。今日の成功と明日の約束の種をまいたのは
彼らなのだから。

_____

_____

_____

40

The best stories come from the worst of times.
Mine challenging times for lessons that will make you
better, stronger, and wiser.

最悪の時にこそ最高のストーリーが生まれる。組織が
不振にあえいだ時代の話を掘り起し、そこから教訓を
得て、より強く賢明な、すぐれた組織に進化しよう。

_____

_____

_____

41

Who amazes and inspires you?
The moment you feel like giving up just think
about them and act as they would in your situation.

驚きと感動を与えてくれる人々は誰だろう?
物事を投げ出したくなった時、彼らだったら
その状況にどう対処するかを考えて行動しよう。

_____

_____

_____

42

Inspiring leaders are those who live up to their organization's ideals amidst challenges, setbacks, and turbulent changes.

逆境や後退、激動の状況にあっても、組織の理想を
目指して困難に立ち向かうリーダーこそ、
人々に勇気を与える真のリーダーである。

_____

_____

_____

43

When you fail, look to great temporary failures
of the past and keep going! Failure isn't a stop sign,
it's a sign of progress.

失敗しても、偉大な先人の一時的な失敗例を
思い返して、あきらめずに前進せよ。失敗は
「止まれ」の標識ではなく、進歩のあかしなのだ。

44

Ask people to share how they've overcome their most
difficult challenges. Learn from each other's
experiences. Grow together.

最も困難な状況を打開した時の体験談を皆と
語り合い、そこから学び合おう。ともに成長しよう。

Share the AHA messages from this book socially by going to
http://aha.pub/InspiredOrgCultures

Section IV
Nourish Your Organization's Culture

An organization's culture is made visible through behavior, and that behavior is driven by assumptions, beliefs, and patterned thinking, in addition to the conscious choices that we make to perpetuate that culture. While leaders often spend time on org charts and strategy, their organizational culture—sometimes disparagingly referred to as "the touchy-feely stuff"—is all too frequently left to chance.

As my mentor, Dr. Edgar Schein, has taught me, organizational culture has both an internal side (how we get along, how we do things) and an external side (what we do to survive and grow, including strategy and tactics). Culture infuses both through our deeper assumptions about who we are, our collective identity, and our sense of our brand.

It can be helpful to think about organizational culture as a kind of "internal brand." A brand is a promise. Most organizations carefully consider what their brand broadcasts externally, but what is the promise that your brand communicates to your people? In the same way that customers have expectations based on brand image, an organization's culture creates expectations in current and potential employees.

An authentic *external* brand must be built on an *internal* organizational culture that is aligned with that brand, otherwise it's just hollow marketing hype. Attempts to dictate your organization's culture through brochures, posters, websites, and coffee mugs bearing empty slogans produce little more than cynicism.

Nourish and strengthen what matters most—that priceless, yet intangible, asset called "organizational culture"—the invisible water in which you and everyone else in your organization swim.

45

Your organization's culture is the invisible water in which you swim. It's what's left when there's nobody left to blame.

組織の文化は見えない水のようなもので、その中で人は泳いでいる。文化こそ、責めを負うべき人が誰もいなくなった後に残るものだ。

_____

_____

_____

46

A brand is a promise. Externally, brand shapes your customers' expectations. What does your cultural brand promise your employees?

ブランドとは「約束」である。組織の対外的なブランドが示す約束によって顧客の期待が決まる。あなたが属する組織の文化のブランドは従業員に何を約束しているか?

_____

_____

_____

47

Establish two or three timeless guiding principles
that will not only serve you in the present,
but also guide future generations.

現在だけでなく将来にも通用し、次の世代を導いて
いける指針を2つ、3つ確立しよう。

_____

_____

_____

48

Your organization's core message must inspire your
people to breathe life into your values. Make it a
message worth remembering.

組織が打ち出す主なメッセージは、人を触発して
組織の価値に命を吹き噲ませられるものでなくては
ならない。心に残るメッセージにしよう。

_____

_____

_____

49

Your organization's culture is the air that your people breathe and the water in which they swim.
It's invisible and omnipresent.

組織の文化は、その中で働く人が吸う空気や、
人が泳ぐ水のようなものだ。文化は目に見えないが、
あらゆるところに存在する。

_____

_____

_____

50

Your brand says a lot about you. It reflects your organization's culture and DNA. It shapes how people perceive your business.

組織が有するブランドは
組織の文化とDNAを反映したものであり、
世間がその組織をどう見ているかの表れである。

_____

_____

_____

51

Every decision you make today influences what you can be tomorrow. Are your decisions taking you closer to your desired future?

組織で今下される決定はすべて、組織の将来の姿に
影響を及ぼす。あなたが属する組織の意思決定は、
目指す将来像に近づくのに役立っているか?

_____

_____

_____

52

An organization's culture embodies nonnegotiable core values, the behavioral norms you'd fire your best person for violating.

組織の文化は中核的価値観の表れであり、
その行動規範に違反する者は優秀な人材でも解雇する
覚悟が要るほどに妥協を許さない価値観である。

_____

_____

_____

53

For an individual to be successful, we must know and
understand our identity, purpose, and goals. The same
goes for organizations.

個人が成功するには、自らのアイデンテイテイ、
目的、目標を認識し、理解しなくてはならない。
組織の成功についても同じである。

_____

_____

_____

54

It's not enough to impose slogans and buzzwords on your people. This induces cynicism. Include them in creating a shared culture.

組織で働く人々にスローガンやもったいぶった言葉を押しつけても冷笑をかうだけだ。彼らを巻き噫んで共通の文化を創り出そう。

_____

_____

_____

55

While your competitors are busy attending to the "tyranny of the urgent," focus on building core values and guiding principles.

競合他社が「緊急性の暴虐」に振り回されている間に、中核的価値観を築き、指針を作ることに注力しよう。

_____

_____

_____

56

Skepticism and Cynicism flourish in organizations with toxic cultures. Don't let this happen to you. Make culture a priority.

不健全な文化を持つ組織には懐疑心と皮肉な考えがはびこる。そんな事態に組織を陥らせてはならない。確固たる文化を築くことを優先させよ。

_____

_____

_____

57

An organization's culture is a mirror reflecting what really matters most to your people. What does your reflection say?

組織の文化は、そこで働く人々にとって本当に重要なことは何かを映し出す鏡である。自分の属する組織の鏡を見てみよう。何が映っているだろう?

_____

_____

_____

58

Determine which attitude to change to attain better altitude, or else your organization will end up at the bottom – in solitude.

組織をさらなる成功の高みに導くため、
人々の取り組みの姿勢をどう改めるべきか決めよう。
それを怠れば組織はどん底に転落し、取り残されるだろう。

_____

_____

_____

59

Making decisions is easier if you know your purpose and your destination. Purpose provides direction and a reason to survive.

めざす目的と目的地がわかっていれば意思決定は
容易になる。目的によって方向性が示され、
組織が生き残るべき理由が明らかになる。

_____

_____

_____

60

Every organization needs to decide the identity that they want to establish and be known for, and then live up to that ideal.

組織は自らが望むアイデンテイテイ、それによって
世に知られたいアイデンテイテイを定め、
その理想に向かって邁進すべきだ。

_____

_____

_____

61

Your customers' perceptions of your organization strongly contribute to building a credible identity for your entity.

あなたの属する組織を顧客の観点でとらえた姿が、組織の確固たるアイデンテイテイ形成に大きく役立つ。

_____

_____

_____

62

Eyes cannot see the values of your organization,
but they can be felt by the human heart.
How does your culture make people feel?

組織が持つ価値観は目に見えないが、人間の心は
それを感じとることができる。あなたが属する組織の
文化は人にどんな印象を与えているだろう？

_____

_____

_____

Share the AHA messages from this book socially by going to
http://aha.pub/InspiredOrgCultures

Section V
Act as Your Organization's Finest Cultural Ambassador

Organizational culture and cultural DNA are far more effective tools for transformational change than a revised strategic plan or an updated org chart. Reorganizations are sometimes cynically referred to as "rearranging the deck chairs on the *Titanic*," and many strategic plans do little more than gather dust. If you're a leader committed to increasing your organization's chances of success, become an organizational culture ambassador.

Whether you're an individual contributor, a manager, an executive, or the CEO, you influence your organization's culture on a daily basis via your behavior. Just as one exasperating jerk can ruin the workday for dozens of people, the example that you set with your behavior and communication can create a pocket of excellence that will inevitably impact everyone who crosses your path.

I sincerely hope that neither country culture nor organizational culture is an unchangeable force field that keeps us locked into ineffective and unproductive ways of working together. Although resistance to change is legendary, my own personal experience is that even one individual can have a significant positive impact on the culture of an organization. You can "lead from any chair," without regard to position or title, by being an example for others.

In my experience, no one feels that they are to blame for a dysfunctional culture, but everyone is responsible for changing it. Start where you are. Begin today to be a role model for others. Change happens one courageous act at a time. Get busy!

63

With every act, you contribute to your organization's culture. It's up to you what you create and how you will be remembered.

人は日々の行動によって組織の文化に貢献する。
あなたが何を創り出すか、何によって皆の記憶に
残るかは、自分しだいだ。

64

An organization's culture is a reflection of who you are. Is it what you want to be? Is it how you want people to think of you?

組織の文化はその組織の姿を反映している。
自分たちの目指す姿になっているか?
世間の人々にこう認識してもらいたいと思う姿に
なっているだろうか?

65

No one feels responsible for a dysfunctional culture.
Own it! Your words and actions make a difference.
Don't be "talk-sick"!

組織の文化がうまく機能していない場合に責任を
取りたがる人はいない。当事者意識を持とう。
あなたの言葉と行動が変革のきっかけとなる。
文句ばかり言っていないで事を起こそう。

_____

_____

_____

66

Regardless of what anyone else does, you have the power
to shape your organization's culture through your behavior
and decisions.

他人がどんな行動を取ろうと、あなたは自らの行動と
決定によって組織の文化を形成する力を持つ。

_____

_____

_____

67

An organization's culture is created by
myriad small acts. What small change
today could make a big difference tomorrow?

組織の文化は数多くの小さな行動の積み重ねで
できていく。今起きている小さな変化のうちどれが、
将来の大きな変革につながるだろう?

_____

_____

_____

68

An organization's culture is constantly shaped by the behaviors of the individuals involved. How are you shaping and evolving it?

組織の文化は、そこで働く個々人の行動に常に影響を受けて形成されていく。その文化の形成と進化にあなたはどんな影響を与えているか?

_____

_____

_____

69

You can't hide your organization's culture from others, it's visible in every interaction with each person you touch. Make magic!

組織の文化を世間の目から隠すことはできない。文化は外部の人々とのやりとりにおのずと現れるからだ。がんばろう!

_____

_____

_____

70

Be an example of what's possible. Behave and speak in ways that would transform your organization if everyone acted as you do.

「やればできる」ことを自ら手本となって示せ。
他の人々があなたと同じように話し、行動すれば、
組織の変革につながる。

_____

_____

_____

71

Find a memorable way to convey your organization's
DNA so you don't lead your people astray.
This is how to lead today! Yay!

自分が属する組織のDNAを伝える方法を見つけよう。
後に続く人を道に迷わせないよう、記憶に残る方法で
伝えよう。現代のリーダーシップはそうあるべきだ。

_____

_____

_____

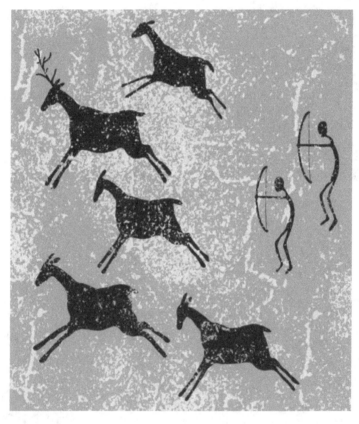

Share the AHA messages from this book socially by going to
http://aha.pub/InspiredOrgCultures

Section VI
Spread Your Organization's Culture
& DNA Through Stories

While abstract in concept, an organization's culture is made visible through the stories that people tell—the good, the bad, and the ugly. Left to evolve on their own these stories won't necessarily strengthen your culture. Fear, uncertainty, and confusion can be spread as easily as hope and possibility. At a Wiefling family vacation my brother read a heartwarming poem about what it meant to be a Wiefling. Honestly, I didn't remember our childhood being all that much fun. But he was extremely skillful in choosing which stories to tell and which to leave out. And I definitely preferred his version to what I remember!

Our past is a doorway, not a prison. To positively impact your organization's culture, highlight stories that create a shared sense of identity, and that demonstrate behaviors aligned with your organization's highest and best aspirations. Inspiring stories can create coherence among even globally diverse and dispersed teams. Where team cohesion is strong, individual behaviors naturally tend to align with this shared identity without the need for excessive direction, rules, and oversight.

What stories from the past have the power to unite and inspire everyone in your organization? What stories from the present showcase those who are living, breathing examples of your organization's core values? What future stories would you like people to be telling about your organization 100 years from now?

Spread your organization's culture and cultural DNA by sharing powerful stories from the past, present, and future. One inspiring story is worth one thousand fact-filled Power Point decks! As I often say about Power Point, "I don't feel the power, and I don't see the point!"

72

Communicate your culture through stories. No one remembers the population of Paris, they remember that Paris is the city of love.

組織の文化を伝えるためにストーリーを語ろう。
人はパリの人口がどのぐらいかを忘れても、
パリが恋の都であることは憶えているものだ。

_____

_____

_____

73

Every organization has a history. Spread the stories that inspire people and bring the core values of your organization to life.

どんな組織にも歴史がある。人々を鼓舞する
ストーリーを広め、組織の中核的価値観に
命を吹き噎もう。

_____

_____

_____

74

Create a living legacy that will be passed on to future generations by discovering, sharing, and preserving your people's stories.

組織で働く人々の物語を発見し、共有し、保存する
ことにより、未来の世代に受け継がれる生きた遺産を
築こう。

_____

_____

_____

75

Tell stories that showcase behaviors your organization values. You can learn from weaknesses, but you can't build on weakness.

組織が重要視する行動のあり方を描いたストーリーを語りつごう。自らの弱みから学ぶことはできても、弱みを土台にして成長することはできない。

_____

_____

_____

76

Sharing stories about what matters most increases the sense of commitment of each member to your organization's greater purpose.

組織にとって一番大切なことは何かを伝えるストーリーを共有することで、組織の大目的に対する各人のコミットメントの意識が高まる。

_____

_____

_____

77

Shared stories are a mirror in which your people can see themselves at their very best. Make time and space for sharing stories.

共有されたストーリーは、
自分の一番よい姿が映し出された鏡のようなものだ。
ストーリーを語り合う時間と場を設けよう。

_____

_____

_____

78

Every individual, team, and organization has a story to tell, a story worth passing on to future generations. What's yours?

個人、チーム、組織にはそれぞれ、
未来の世代に語り継ぐ価値のあるストーリーがある。
あなたが伝えたいストーリーは?

_____

_____

_____

79

What stories will be told 100 years from now in your organization? Live today so you are an inspiration for future generations.

組織の中で、100年先まで語りつがれるストーリーは何だろう? 未来の世代によい刺激を与えられる存在となるべく、今を生きよう。

_____

_____

_____

80

What stories of the past could inspire your organization's future? What remarkable legacy hides in your shared history? Find it!

組織にとって、過去のどんなストーリーが未来に
資する刺激となるだろう? 共有された歴史に隠された
すばらしい遺産を探し出そう。

81

How would you like your organization to be perceived and remembered? What headlines would you like to see in the news 100 years from now?

あなたの属する組織の望ましい対外イメージは?
どんな組織として人々の記憶に残りたいか? 100年後の
組織に関するニュースではどんな見出しを期待する
か?

Share the AHA messages from this book socially by going to
http://aha.pub/InspiredOrgCultures

Section VII
Leverage Your Organization's Culture & DNA

The culture of an organization is a system that is far more ubiquitous and powerful than any balanced scorecard or strategy map. And that organizational culture influences everything that is said and done by the people within that system. So, how are organizations leveraging this mighty force? Not very well!

Myriad studies have revealed that most people are not engaged in their work, and the vast majority of managers aren't focusing on their organization's most important priorities. The challenges in globally dispersed organizations are the greatest, with over 80 percent of global teams judging themselves unsuccessful. The root causes of these dire statistics? Completely predictable and preventable issues related to leadership, teams, and organizational culture.

Global teams, for example, break down primarily due to lack of trusting relationships, failure to overcome communication barriers that go far beyond language, a lack of goal alignment, and a non-existent shared team vision. The need for shared goals, effective communication, and trusting relationships might seem like common sense, but the evidence suggests that it's not common practice. Obviously, as Dr. Robert Sutton wrote in his famous book, *The Knowing-Doing Gap*, there's an enormous chasm between knowing and doing.

Better technology and collaboration tools won't bridge this gap. Even co-located teams born in the same country and speaking the same language struggle to overcome these barriers. How can thousands of people spread across dozens of countries and time zones hope to work together as a true team to achieve common goals? By leveraging the unifying power of their shared identity and the genetic roots of their greatness.

As invisible as the air we breathe and as inescapable as gravity, organizational culture is an essential ingredient for achieving and sustaining success. Leverage your organization's culture and cultural DNA to connect your people to a purpose beyond profit, bring your core values to life, and unleash your organization's full potential.

82

Use your DNA as a guide to which of your organization's strengths should be nurtured and preserved into the distant future.

将来に向けて、組織の強みのうちどれを伸ばし、維持するかを決める指針として、組織の DNA を活用しよう。

_____

_____

_____

83

Creating and sustaining a positive organizational culture isn't "touchy feely." It's a proven path to greater profit.

前向きな組織の文化を築き、維持することは、
感情論にもとづいた取り組みではない。
利益増大のための、成功が実証された道筋なのだ。

_____

_____

_____

84

An organization's culture keeps your people unified and focused on the future while massive changes devastate your competition.

競合他社が大きな変化の波に翻弄される一方で、
組織の文化があるおかげで人々は力を合わせ、
将来に向かって前進できる。

85

Others can steal your strategies, but your organization's culture and DNA can't be transplanted. They define what's uniquely you.

戦略は盗まれることがあっても、
組織の文化とDNAは他へ移植できない。
それらは組織の独自性を表すものだからだ。

86

Your organization's culture is a sustainable competitive advantage. Competitors can imitate you, but they'll never duplicate you.

組織の文化は持続可能な競争優位性をもたらす。
競合他社があなたの属する組織の真似をしても、
同じ組織になりかわることはできない。

_____

_____

_____

87

Strengthening your organization's culture creates positive changes that attract and retain great people and promote growth.

組織の文化を強化することでよい変化が
もたらされる。優秀な人材が集まり、定着し、
組織の成長が促される。

_____

_____

_____

88

Your organization's culture and DNA shape the way your people Feel, Act, Communicate, and Think. It's a FACT!

組織の文化とDNAはそこで働く人々の気持ち（F）、
行動（A）、意思疎通（C）、思考（T）に
影響を与える。これが事実（FACT）である！

_____

_____

_____

89

Want truly engaged people who love contributing to the good of your organization? Instill your culture and DNA into their hearts.

組織に喜んで貢献し、
何事にも積極的に関わる人々を求めるなら、
組織の文化とDNAを彼らの心にしみこませよう。

_____

_____

_____

90

Your organization's DNA is a wise filter that enables you to clearly identify what to exclude. Know when to say "no."

組織のDNAは、何を取り除くべきかを決める
判断基準となる有効なフィルターだ。
言うべき時には "No" と言おう。

_____

_____

_____

91

A strong organizational culture builds hope, and research has proven that people with hope set higher goals and perform better.

組織の力強い文化は希望を生む。
人々が希望を持てばより高い目標を掲げ、
業績が上がることは調査でも証明されている。

_____

_____

_____

92

Fewer difficulties in interpersonal relationships and less stress are some of the benefits of a strong organizational culture.

組織の力強い文化が根づくメリットは、
対人関係の問題やストレスが減ることだ。

_____

_____

_____

93

An organization's culture makes it unnecessary to manage your people. A shared identity inspires the right choices without force.

組織の文化がしっかりしていれば、
部下をいちいち管理する必要がなくなる。
共通のアイデンティティに刺激を受けた人々は、
強制されなくても正しい選択ができるようになる。

94

A healthy organizational culture unleashes the innate talent of each individual, and turns a group of people into a real team.

組織の健全な文化は、
そこで働く個々人の内なる才能を目覚めさせ、
単なる人の集まりから本物のチームに変容させる。

95

If you feel lost on your way to the future, look to the best of your organization's past for inspiration and guidance.

将来へ向かって進む旅の途中、
道に迷ったと感じたら、組織の過去から
指針とひらめきを得ればよい。

96

An organization's culture is a solid foundation for success that goes beyond making a profit to making a difference.

組織の文化は、営利活動を超えて世の中を変える
成功の土台である。

_____

_____

_____

97

A shared understanding of your organization's culture and DNA is essential to bringing your core values to life.

組織の中核的価値観を活かすためには、組織の文化と
DNAに対する理解の浸透が欠かせない。

_____

_____

_____

98

Exploring your organization's DNA together deepens
relationships among team members and strengthens
commitment to each other.

チームメンバーとともに組織のDNAを探ることで
メンバー同士の関係が深まり、
お互いに対するコミットメントが強まる。

_____

_____

_____

99

A clear understanding of your organization's DNA is an
excellent guide to which qualities to preserve and which
need to evolve.

組織のDNAを明確に理解することで、どの特性を
残し、どの特性を進化させるべきかが見えてくる。

_____

_____

_____

100

Let your organization's DNA guide you to build a purpose beyond profit, to what's priceless.

利益を超えたかけがえのない目的を打ち立てるに
あたって、組織のDNAを案内役としよう。

_____

_____

_____

101

A healthy organizational culture increases the loyalty of
your customers and your people, increasing the value of
your brand.

組織の健全な文化は、そこで働く人々と顧客の
ロイヤルティを向上させ、ブランド価値を高める。

_____

_____

_____

Share the AHA messages from this book socially by going to
http://aha.pub/InspiredOrgCultures

Section VIII
Design Your Future Together

Past performance doesn't guarantee future success. Many Fortune 500 companies fall off of that prestigious list every decade. Results in organizations depend on a combination of strategy, structure, and culture.

Organizational culture is created and perpetuated through the cumulative behaviors of leaders, managers, individuals, and teams. The quality of your culture should not be left to chance! Time, attention, and resources must be purposefully directed toward shaping your organization's culture. Unfortunately, no one individual feels responsible for dysfunctional cultural artifacts, and thus it can be difficult to find someone who is willing to step up and lead painful, yet necessary, changes. Leadership is the missing ingredient.

As Dr. Edgar Schein said, "The only thing of real importance that leaders do is to create and manage culture."[2] Regrettably, a study by Strategy&[3] showed that there's plenty of room for improvement here! Strategy& reported that 96 percent of organizations surveyed felt that cultural change was needed in their organization, and 51 percent said that a major cultural overhaul was required. But as anyone who's tried to change their spouse can tell you, changing behavior is no easy task. Simply describing the desired behaviors and the "case for change" is insufficient. If logic alone were enough to convince people to change, no one would smoke cigarettes!

Don't just slap a propaganda poster on the wall. Hanging a sign that says "Cat" over a doghouse won't suddenly make your golden retriever meow, hunt mice,

---

2. Edgar Schein, quote in John Kispert, "Want to Innovate? It Starts with Your Corporate Culture," *The Management Blog (BloombergBusinessweek*blog), October 23, 2013, http://www.businessweek.com/articles/2013-10-23/jumpstart-innovation-by-transforming-corporate-culture.
3. DeAnne Aguirre, Rutger von Post, and Micah Alpern, "Culture's role in enabling organizational change: Survey ties transformation success to deft handling of cultural issues," *Strategy&*, November 14, 2013, http://www.strategyand.pwc.com/ media/file/Strategyand_Cultures-Role-in-Enabling-Organizational-Change.pdf.

or go crazy for catnip. Lead your team on a cultural change expedition! Leap into your organization's future together and vividly imagine the possibilities. What stories do you hope to tell about your organization next year? In 10 years? A hundred years from now?

Dreaming is a form of planning. I've personally experienced the power of "thinking from the future" to clarify how an organization needs to learn, grow, and evolve *today* in order to bring that future into existence. Dreaming must be followed by action, but dreams come first.

102

If you want to create a better future for
your organization, shape your destiny.
Don't let the past dictate your future.

組織のよりよい未来を築きたければ、運命を自ら形づ
くろう。過去に縛られ未来を描けないようではだめ
だ。

_____

_____

_____

103

What will your organization be like 50 or 100 years from now? Will it still exist or will it be extinct? Strong cultures persist!

あなたの属する組織は今から50年後、100年後に
どうなっているだろう?
存続しているか、消滅しているか?
生き残るのは力強い文化だ。

_____

_____

_____

104

To enhance your organization's culture, invest in the professional and personal development of every member of your team.

組織の文化を強化するには、チームメンバー全員の
公私両方の育成に投資すべきだ。

_____

_____

_____

105

Don't be satisfied with survival. Dare to make a difference. Create a reputation that will be both inspiring and motivating.

組織がただ存続しているだけで満足してはならない。
世の中を変える勇気を持て。人を鼓舞し、
意欲を起こさせる組織だという評判を確立せよ。

_____

_____

_____

106

Every interaction is an opportunity to contribute to the history of your organization. Make wise choices.
Live a great story!

人々と交流するたび、組織の歴史に貢献できる機会が生まれる。賢い選択をしよう。
後人のためにすばらしいストーリーを残そう。

_____

_____

_____

107

Don't rely on rules and force to keep people aligned.
Create a tangible organizational culture that evokes the
desired behaviors.

組織内の整合性をとるために人をルールで縛っては
いけない。望ましい行動を引き出すような
組織の文化を作り上げ、目に見える形で示そう。

_____

_____

_____

108

Your organization's DNA should continuously evolve
through personal growth, building community,
and challenging the status quo.

組織のDNAは、人の成長、コミュニティの構築、
現状への挑戦を通じて進化し続けるべきだ。

_____

_____

_____

109

Your assumptions and beliefs about the future determine the actions your organization will take now to achieve your vision.

将来のビジョン実現のために組織が今とるべき
行動は、内部の人々の仮説と信念によって決まる。

110

Reflect on your cultural DNA when you lose your way. You'll find clues that will restore clarity and get you back on track.

道に迷った時、組織の文化のDNAを思い起こそう。
再び視界が開けて、軌道修正できるヒントが
見つかるだろう。

111

Don't let others decide who or what your organization
should be. Strive to be uniquely and authentically
you in all you say & do.

組織のあり方を第三者に決めさせてはならない。
言葉と行動で組織の独自性を存分に発揮せよ。

_____

_____

_____

112

Focusing only on money? That's like driving with your
eyes glued to the speedometer. To fill your pockets,
fulfill your purpose.

金銭にばかり目を向けることは、スピードメーター
だけを見つめて運転するようなものだ。自らの
ポケツトを満たしたいなら、目的の達成を目指せ。

_____

_____

_____

113

Take responsibility for your organization's future.
Each person contributes to your shared destiny
with every word and deed.

組織の未来に皆で責任を持とう。それぞれの言葉と
行動によって、皆が共有する運命に貢献できる。

_____

_____

_____

114

Create an organizational culture that you and your team
can be proud of. Build a legacy that will outlast the
Great Pyramids!

自分とチームメンバーが誇りに思える組織の文化を
作り上げよう。ピラミッドをしのぐほどに長く残る
遺産を築くのだ。

_____

_____

_____

115

The choices and decisions you make today determine the kind of future you'll have tomorrow. What kind of future are you creating?

今日の選択と決定が組織の明日の姿を決める。
あなたはどんな未来を創るだろう?

_____

_____

_____

116

Small changes can make a big difference. Don't try to boil the ocean! Each courageous act enhances your organization's culture.

小さな変化の積み重ねが大きな変革につながる。大げさな手段に走ろうとするな。勇気ある行動の一つ一つが組織の文化を育んでいく。

117

Determine which aspects of your DNA and culture to keep and which to change to steer toward a brighter future. Change is a choice!

組織のDNAと文化のどの要素を残し、どの要素を変えるかを決め、明るい未来に向けて進んでいこう。変化とは一つの選択なのだ。

118

Culture can feel like invisible cement,
but everything changes. Find ways to evolve
your DNA in order to survive and thrive.

文化が目に見えないセメントの壁のように感じられる
こともあるだろうが、どんなものでも変わっていく。
生き残って繁栄するために、組織のDNAを進化させる
方法を見つけ出すのだ。

_____

_____

_____

119

In search of excellence? Invest in your organization's
culture or you'll find yourself knee deep in excrement!

卓越した成果を求めるなら、組織の文化に投資せよ。
さもなければ泥沼にはまって身動きがとれなくなる。

_____

_____

_____

Share the AHA messages from this book socially by going to
http://aha.pub/InspiredOrgCultures

Section IX
Grow Together

Two good friends working in a garage in Palo Alto started a company together. In the early days that company established "The HP Way," which became legendary as an example of a healthy, vibrant organizational culture. But a founder's spirit is often lost over time, and growth through M&A often results in a sewn-together culture akin to Dr. Frankenstein's monster. How can a bunch of people separated by borders, boundaries, and barriers of every kind feel truly connected? By exploring and strengthening their shared organizational culture and cultural DNA.

If you study *country* cultures you'll inevitably stumble across the "iceberg model." Visible above the waterline are the obvious traits and behaviors often associated with a stereotype of a particular culture. Walk down a busy Tokyo street during lunchtime and you can't help but notice the sea of dark suits, white shirts, and dark ties. In the evening, you might wonder how such "shy and conservative" businessmen can keep so many karaoke joints in business. Only a peek below the surface can resolve this seeming contradiction. Below the water level you'll find the less obvious influencers of behavior—factors an outsider would likely miss in a casual encounter. These values, beliefs, and norms, and the observable behaviors that spring from them, are what cross-cultural experts refer to as a country's "culture."

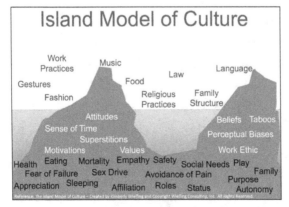

The Island Model of Culture

After working with people from over 50 different countries, I find the iceberg model inadequate to describe the extensive common ground that all human beings share. Beneath our obvious differences and obscure motivations lies the bedrock of our shared humanity. An island model seems like a much more suitable metaphor because it reveals how we are all connected at a deeper level. Applied to organizations, this island model can be used to motivate us to dig deeper, far beneath the superficial, to discover the common ground upon which we can build a shared future.

Diversity is an advantage, but if you want to grow together you must explore what you have in common below the waterline—your shared organizational culture and cultural DNA.

120

Teams who clearly understand and commit to their core purpose, and embrace a shared identity, are the most invincible. Wooohoooo!

チームの主な目的をはっきり理解し、共通の
アイデンティティを信じて全力で取り組むチームは
向かうところ敵なしだ。最高じゃないか!

_____

_____

_____

121

An organization's culture is a valuable guide to choosing behaviors that align with your values and support your vision.

組織の価値観に合致し、ビジョンを支える行動を選ぶ時、価値ある指針となるのが組織の文化である。

_____

_____

_____

122

There's nothing more rewarding than seeing your people live and breathe your organization's culture in pursuit of its purpose.

組織の目的を追求するにあたって、メンバーが組織の文化を自分のものにして実践している姿を見る時ほど、報われたと感じられる瞬間はない。

_____

_____

_____

123

Once your organizational culture is clearly understood by everyone involved it becomes an effective and powerful engine for growth.

組織の文化は、関係者全員が明確に理解すれば、強力で効果的な成長のエンジンとなる。

_____

_____

_____

124

Each individual possesses a unique set of gifts. Match each one with the place where they can contribute best and let them shine!

人はそれぞれ独自の才能を持っている。
その才を活かして最大の貢献ができる職につかせ、
実力を発揮させよう!

_____

_____

_____

125

An organization's culture shapes the values and behaviors
that enable your people to collaborate effortlessly and
effectively.

組織の文化は、メンバー間の容易かつ効果的な協業を
可能にする価値観と行動を形づくるものである。

126

You may not be able to change your organization's past,
but it's never too late to do something about your
present culture.

組織の過去は変えられないかもしれないが、
今の組織の文化を変えるのに遅すぎる
ということはない。

127

The more you engage in dialogue about your organization's culture, the stronger it becomes. Conversation creates reality.

組織の文化について対話をすればするほど
文化は強固になり、可能性が現実味を帯びてくる。

_____

_____

_____

128

The journey to future possibilities begins when each member of your team fully understands your organization's reason for being.

あなたのチームメンバー全員が
組織の存在理由について完全に理解した時、
将来の可能性へ向かう旅が始まる。

_____

_____

_____

129

Behaviors must align with an organization's core values.
Define what's aligned, and support clear consequences
for misalignment.

組織のメンバーの行動は組織の中核的価値観と
整合性がとれていなくてはならない。
整合性のとれた行動とは何かを定義し、
それに反した行動の結果起きることに対応せよ。

130

Truly great organizations are those that are unified by
their organization's culture, not governed by strict
policies and rules.

真に偉大な組織は、共通の文化により
一丸となっている組織であって、
厳格な方針や規則で統治されている組織ではない。

131

Be the kind of organization that will inspire generations to come. Make what you stand for worthy and unforgettable.

今後何世代にもわたって人を鼓舞し続ける組織であれ。
組織の目的を記憶に残る、価値あるものにせよ。

132

Start with the basics—your organization's history, what you value beyond profit, and your big crazy dreams for the future.

基礎から始めよ―自分が属する組織の沿革を調べ、
利益より価値あるものについて語り、
途方もない夢を思い描け。

133

Make time to strengthen your organizational culture.
It's never your most urgent work, but it is your most
important work.

時間を作って、組織の文化の強化に取り組もう。
最も緊急度が高いとは言えないが、
あなたにとって最も重要度の高い仕事だ。

_____

_____

_____

134

Every organization looks like a separate island in an ocean, but deep down they all share the common ground of human beingness.

組織はそれぞれ海に浮かぶ独立した島のように
見えるが、深く掘り下げてみると
人間味を感じさせる共通の基盤がある。

_____

_____

_____

135

Every organization has a history. What's yours? Learn it. Share it. Build on its strengths. Tell your story to the world.

どの組織にも歴史がある。あなたの属する組織の
歴史を学び、共有し、強みを活かして事を進めよう。
組織独自のストーリーを世界に向けて発信しよう。

_____

_____

_____

136

Your organization's culture is the foundation of opportunities that will help your team grow and your organization prosper.

組織の文化はチームを成長させ、組織の繁栄に
役立つチャンスをもたらす基盤である。

_____

_____

_____

137

Appreciate and celebrate what you value. What's rewarded gets repeated. An attitude of gratitude beats a band of critics.

組織の価値観を大切にし、喜び合おう。人は
自分の行為が高く評価されればその行為を繰り返す。
批判ばかりするより感謝の姿勢で事に当たろう。

_____

_____

_____

138

An organization's true culture springs from the authentic commitment of each individual to a purpose beyond financial gain.

組織の文化は、そこで働く人々一人ひとりの決意から生まれる。金銭的な利得を超えた目的に本気で取り組む人々が真の文化をつくる。

_____

_____

_____

139

Each office, region, or team may seem like isolated islands, but deep below the surface all are connected through a shared culture.

それぞれ独立した島々のように見えがちなオフィス、地域、チームだが、深いところでは共通の文化を通じてつながっている。

_____

_____

_____

140

When people share the same sense of identity, they remain
strong and united. When the shared story falls apart,
so does the team.

アイデンテイテイについて
共通の感覚を持つ人々のチームは強く、結束が固い。
共有したストーリーが崩れれば、チームも崩壊する。

Wiefling Consulting
Conceive it. Believe it. Achieve it.

Appendix:

This is the article that Kimberly first wrote that inspired the writing of this book.

The Stories We Tell—Creating and Nurturing Your Organization's Culture & DNA

Kimberly Wiefling, Wiefling Consulting, Inc.
kimberly@wiefling.com +1 650 867 0847

Thanks to Cinda Voeglti and DeAnna Burghardt, this article was originally published on http://www.projectconnections.com.

Recently, several of my clients have become extremely interested in exploring what they call their "corporate DNA." At first, I resisted because I was concerned that this metaphor implied that they were incapable of changing. But for the most part, this model is being used to explore the unique identity of an organization—the historical strengths that are admired and should be preserved and transmitted to future generations.

Most every kid who has the luxury of getting an education learns the basics of DNA. It's what causes a giraffe to have a long neck, kangaroos to have pouches, and porcupines to have quills instead of fur. Tadpoles turn into frogs, not butterflies. And much of behavior has its roots in an organism's DNA. Birds have wings, but dogs don't; therefore, dogs don't fly. Snakes, lacking both legs and wings, resort to crawling. But what is the meaning of the DNA of an organization?

If you look up "corporate DNA" on Wikipedia, you›ll be redirected to an article on "organizational culture." Here's how organizational culture and cultural DNA are related.

Organizational culture is «the way we are» today, including the laundry list of do's and don'ts that old-timers share with newbies on their first day of work. It's "the way we do things around here," even if we've forgotten why we're doing them. It's the collection of observable patterns in an organization at the present time. People naturally assume that these patterns will continue into the future. And they probably will, unless the organization experiences a deep, sometimes radical, change. Organizational culture is made visible through behavior, and behavior is driven by assumptions, beliefs, and patterned thinking, in addition to the conscious choices we make to perpetuate that culture. As my mentor, Dr. Edgar Schein, has taught me, organizational culture has both an internal side—how we get along, how we do things—and an external side—what we do to survive and grow, including our strategy and tactics. Culture infuses both the internal and external through the deeper assumptions of who we are, our identity, and our sense of our brand based on our history.

Organizational DNA is a property of the culture and is the historical basis of why we behave this way—the genetic code at the root of these behaviors. Like the DNA of birds and snakes, it influences whether our organization will fly or crawl. Although we can change our behaviors radically, our DNA establishes some boundaries. A dog that's been abused might bark aggressively or bite humans, but it won't start eating worms, tweeting, or building a nest out of twigs!

Culture as Internal Brand. One useful way to think about organizational culture is as your internal brand. A brand is a promise. Most companies carefully consider what their brand communicates externally, but what is the brand promise your company makes to your employees? In the same way that customers have expectations based on brand image, your organizational culture creates expectations in your employees. I strongly believe that an authentic external brand must be based on an organizational culture with which it is aligned.

DNA Isn't Destiny. As a scientist, I worry that DNA as a metaphor for corporate identity isn't technically accurate. People frequently talk about their organization's DNA as if it can't, or shouldn't, be changed. Some executives proudly speak of their corporate history as if their future is determined primarily by their past. Before we embrace this metaphor, there are a few things we should know about DNA.

1. DNA in nature isn't forever fixed nor does it unalterably determine what happens in the life of an organism. Mutations occur naturally, scientists intentionally create genetic modifications, and reproductive processes combine genes in ways that create new and sometimes surprising results, like the baby "zonkey" in this picture. (See more fascinating hybrids here.) Similarly, organizations that grow through mergers and acquisitions must integrate the combined DNA of previously distinct entities.

2. Most genetic code isn't expressed. For example, over 98 percent of <u>human genetic material</u> is so-called «<u>non-coding DNA</u>.» This DNA isn't junk! It's important to regulating and protecting the genome, but it doesn't directly dictate our development as human beings. A parallel in organizations is the importance of focusing on stories and examples that bring us together around our shared purpose and selectively forgetting what doesn't contribute to a better future.

3. Environmental factors like <u>temperature and light can impact gene expression</u>. For example, Thomas Hunt Morgan's <u>Experimental Zoology</u> reports that genetically identical caterpillars exposed to different colors of light during their chrysalis stage develop dramatic differences in wing color. Likewise, organizations are subject to external influences, and some (<u>but not most</u>) do find ways to break free of their historical roots, rather than continue unproductive trends, and therefore avoid becoming extinct.

4. Here is yet more evidence that we are not slaves to our DNA: "<u>Lipton</u> believes the old paradigm of 'genetic determinism' is being replaced with the idea that genes respond to information—both external environments and cognitive (internal) environments." Gene expression is impacted by the context in which they exist.

In spite of my scientific misgivings, I've found that exploring the DNA of an organization can be an extremely effective way to create a shared sense of identity among even globally diverse, dispersed teams. Groups with a clear understanding of their shared core identity and the kinds of behaviors that naturally spring from this understanding form more cohesive teams. Individual behaviors tend to naturally align with this team identity, without the need for direction, rules, and oversight.

If you want to discover your organization's cultural DNA and use it to unite your team, don't rush over to your PR department to pick up a stack of those glossy brochures containing the company history and poignant stories of the founders. I know managers who have hundreds of these tree-killers stashed in their office. Giving them out provokes cynicism and pretty much guarantees they'll go straight into the recycling bin.

Here are three powerful and engaging exercises that I've found to be much more effective than handing out brochures. It's all about stories. (People remember stories, as Chip and Dan Heath explained in *Made to Stick*.) If you want a message to change the results you're getting in your team, it must be Heard, Understood, Remembered, and Acted upon (HURrAh!), so I strongly recommend using stories as the basis of your DNA discussions. But those stories must be shared and talked about, not just read in a pamphlet. A story-based "DNA expedition" will generate increased loyalty to your company and inspire behavior that aligns with shared values discovered during your cultural DNA session.

The Founders and Key Moments in Your History. The first stories to explore are those of the people who founded your organization. Their stories often inspire admiration because of their courageous risk taking, determination, or staunch commitment to something beyond making a profit. Here are a few of my favorite examples:

- Suntory - In 1899, Shinjiro Torii opened a wine shop in Osaka, Japan, and then proceeded to make a popular port wine domestically. Later, Suntory was the first to distill whiskey in Japan. Of course, many people believed that it was impossible to make a great whiskey in Japan, but his "Yatte Minahare!" spirit (roughly translated, "Go for It!") prevailed.

- Kuraray - Magosaburō Ōhara founded this company in 1926, and his son, Soichiro Ohara, has continued the legacy of "contributing to the world and individual well-being through actions that others are unable to produce." This would be just a slogan on a website if it weren't for my personal experience working with Kuraray for the past ten years. I find myself quoting Mr. Ohara's advice to teams locked in an unproductive pattern of "death by consensus." He famously said, "If we wait until everyone agrees, it's too late! We must take action when only two or three executives agree." Indeed!

- Yamaha - In 1887, Torakusu Yamaha built his first reed organ and hand-carried it over the mountains to the music university in Tokyo, where it was flatly rejected due to its poor tuning. Undaunted, he created an improved version and carried it once again on this torturous journey. This organ became the foundation of the Yamaha music business.

- Hewlett-Packard - The friendship forged by Bill Hewlett and Dave Packard in 1934 was the basis of a legendary company. I was fortunate enough to work there for ten years while Bill and Dave were still a palpable presence in the form of *The HP Way*. As an idealistic young person who believed the stories in those glossy brochures, I felt it was my personal responsibility to live up to the legacy that these two gentlemen had created. This resulted in an annual chastisement in my performance reviews: "Kimberly has unrealistically high expectations for herself and others." Yup! Got that right! But it was Bill and Dave's high expectations that I felt I was living up to, not my own.

In addition to studying the adventures of the founders, review significant internal and external stories that punctuate the company's history. Tales of expansion, new product launches, and other successes are valuable, but so are stories of perseverance during difficult times, as well as how people behaved when facing overwhelming challenges and setbacks.

EXERCISE #1 - "Explore Your Past"

- Prepare in advance by having each person read relevant stories from your organization's past. In addition, ask people to think of stories from their own work experience that demonstrate your cultural DNA at its very best.

- Sitting in a circle, have each person share a story that had the most positive impact on them and explain why it impacted them.

- Have everyone in the group jot down on sticky notes—writing BIG—a keyword or two that captures the "essence" of the company's identity from each story.

- Place these sticky notes on flipcharts in the center of the circle as shown in this picture.

- Next, create a collage by combining these words with pictures that capture this essence in a way that words alone cannot describe. Ask participants to bring magazines and other pictures that express the cultural DNA, or use a set of pictures like CCL's Visual Explorer Cards.

- Doing this activity silently is particularly useful for teams where people don't share mastery of a common language.

- Play some music in the background to set the mood!

Piece these collages together to create a patchwork quilt that vividly conveys your cultural DNA. Don't just throw them away when the exercise is over! Preserve and share them widely.

If the collage activity is just too "arts and crafts-y" for your people, try this variation:

- Gather in small teams around white boards and together, silently draw a picture that captures the essence of these stories. Then have each team present their team drawing without preparation. What essential qualities and characteristics of your organization's culture were demonstrated through their drawings and presentations? Encourage

the entire group to discuss the key qualities of your culture that was demonstrated by each team's interpretation.

Here are guidelines for useful discussions to follow the above exercises:

- Discuss what will survive into the far future. What will still be "core" fifty years from now? Determine which of these qualities and characteristics should be passed on to future generations and preserved for the long-term future of your organization.

- Brainstorm how these core cultural elements serve as guiding principles in your business today. What stories from your own experience align with these principles? What other situations are you facing that could benefit from the values and behaviors modeled in these stories? How can we demonstrate the very best of our collective past through our own behaviors in the present?

Sharing and discussing these stories as a team can produce powerful insights about what is admired and valued in your organization, and influence people to behave similarly.

Who We Are NOT! In general, people seem to find it easier to think from a negative perspective, and the next exercise directly appeals to that tendency. This is a fabulously fun exercise and one that even engineers enjoy. Ideally, you should do it right after the first exercise.

EXERCISE #2 - "This Will Never Happen Here!"

- Break into teams of three or four people.
- Gather at flip charts and brainstorm the following categories:
  - Products that you will NEVER make
  - Services that you will NEVER offer
  - News headlines you will NEVER see about your organization
  - Advertising slogans that you will NEVER use
  - Famous people you will NEVER feature in advertising about your organization
  - Behavior and language you will NEVER witness at work

You can also add other categories for this brainstorm that are relevant to your business. One of my clients, famous for adventurous outdoor sports equipment, had a terrific time with this one. Rest assured, they are never going to make «senior diapers,» their slogan won›t ever be, "You're in good hands," and Lady Gaga will never get an offer to promote their extreme sports products.

You can take this exercise one step further by reversing each of these "NEVERS" to discover who you are, your values, your strategies, and what your organization values most.

Remember the Future. Dreamers and scenario planners have been using this technique for years. Jump into the future and vividly imagine a possibility, and then explore what that scenario implies about the behavior and choices required today to bring that future into existence. This exercise will set the stage for you and your team to be "Cultural DNA Ambassadors," spreading the best of your identity to everyone who comes into contact with you.

EXERCISE #3 - "Imagining Your Future"

- Imagine it's fifty years from now and you have long since retired. What will be your legacy? What stories do you hope people in your organization will tell about you and your team?

- Self-organize into small groups and create "stories from the future." For example, you might imagine that your company is celebrating the fifty-year anniversary of the launch of your amazing product or service. Or, perhaps 100 newly hired employees are crammed into a room to watch a video about how your team tackled and overcame seemingly impossible challenges. What do you hope they will be saying as they discuss your historical stories?

- Present your stories as a "news report from the future," complete with roving reporters, satellite links to remote locations, and interviews of some of your now-retired team members. Don't skimp on the drama! Set up a news desk, get some pretend microphones (a rubber chicken works great for this), and ham it up! Imagining the future is the first step to creating it!

Just reading about this exercise doesn't even come close to the experience of living it. Don't underestimate the creativity of your team! I've done this exercise with all kinds of people in all kinds of jobs, from executives to engineers, and everyone—including the stodgiest curmudgeons—totally loves it.

Your Future Cultural DNA Is in Your Hands. For better or worse, today's workplace behaviors will become tomorrow's organizational history. As a leader, you are automatically a "Cultural DNA Ambassador." Don't just slap a purpose-vision-mission-values propaganda poster on the wall! Hanging a big sign over the doghouse door that reads, "You are a cat," won't suddenly make your golden retriever meow, hunt mice, or go crazy for catnip.

And don't allow yourself be trapped by your organization's past! You might have been born with straight black hair, but you can dye it platinum blond and get a perm if you like. Finally, take advantage of the power of selective forgetting.

> *"Happiness? That's nothing more than health and a poor memory." —Albert Schweitzer*

At a Wiefling family reunion, my brother read a heartwarming poem about what it meant to grow up as a Wiefling. Honestly, I didn't remember our childhood being all that much fun. But he was extremely skillful in choosing which stories to tell and which to leave out. As rough and tumble as our family is, everyone had tears in their eyes by the time he finished. (And I definitely prefer his version over the one I remember!) Our organization's cultural DNA is a doorway, not a prison. The stories we tell influence our beliefs, our thinking, and ultimately, our behaviors. Don't go the way of companies like <u>Enron</u>! Create a shared story that you will be proud to hear told fifty years from now. —Kimberly

Are you determined to transform your organizational culture into a competitive advantage?

Contact Kimberly at: +1 650 867 0847 or <u>Kimberly@wiefling.com</u>

About the Author

Kimberly Wiefling helps organizations achieve what SEEMS impossible, but is *merely* difficult. How? By turning managers into leaders and groups into teams. Her first book, *Scrappy Project Management*, was translated into Japanese by Nikkei Business Press. *Scrappy Women in Business* celebrates women's contributions to the business world through the power of storytelling, both in the book and on the companion website, ScrappyWomen.biz. A physicist by education, Kimberly realized long ago the limits of technology devoid of human skills—the so-called "touchy feely" aspects of working in teams so vital to success, and so frequently overlooked. She facilitates highly engaging transformational workshops based on her "Possibilities Toolbox" (http://wiefling.com/our-services/workshops/), which she developed for the professors of Tokyo Medical and Dental University for use in their human skills curriculum at TMDU. Her intensive behavior-changing "learning laboratories," which she playfully refers to as "workshocks," directly translate into business results. She's worked globally with people from over 50 different countries, and her clients include many well-known global brands in a wide variety of industries. Kimberly is passionate about making a meaningful difference by working with organizations committed to solving the problems of Our World—profitably and thus sustainably.

If you're interested in receiving periodic doses of information and inspiration from me—my so-called "Scrappy Kimberly Kamp"—just send an email to scrappy@kimberlywiefling.com with "Subscribe to Scrappy" in the subject line. Woohoo! EXCITING! – Kimberly

AHAthat™

AHAthat makes it easy to share, author, and promote content. There are over 40,000 quotes (AHAmessages™) by thought leaders from around the world that you can share in seconds for free.

For those who want to author their own book, we have time-tested proven processes that allow you to write your AHAbook™ of 140 digestible, bite-sized morsels in eight hours or less. Once your content is on AHAthat, you have a customized link that you can use to have your fans/advocates share your content and help grow your network.

➲ Start sharing: **http://AHAthat.com**

➲ Start authoring: **http://AHAthat.com/Author**

Please go directly to this book in AHAthat and share each AHAmessage socially at
http://aha.pub/InspiredOrgCultures.

CPSIA information can be obtained
at www.ICGtesting.com
Printed in the USA
FSHW04n1647270218
44925FS